Twelve
Christmas Carols,

BY

RICHARD R. TERRY

TWELVE CHRISTMAS CAROLS.

For Four Voices or Unison.

—

By

RICHARD R. TERRY.

—

Words, XIV Century, chiefly from the Sloane MS.

———•———

CONTENTS.

———•———

Price: Staff, 1/6; Sol-fa, 1/6; Words only, complete, 3d.

TO MY WIFE

(In memory of Christmas, 1909).

PREFACE.

WITH the exception of Miss Guiney's charming verses ("Tryste Noel") the words of these carols are from old sources, chiefly the Sloane MS., A.D. 1396. The spelling has been modernised here and there.

Without discussing Carol "form," it will suffice to say that Christmas words do not make a carol out of what would otherwise be a hymn tune or part-song. In other words, a tune can only be termed a carol the nearer it approximates to the folk-song type and the further it departs from the hymn tune. It ought, moreover, to stand on its own melodic basis independent of harmony.

This collection is a humble attempt to suggest rather than reproduce the characteristics of the old traditional carols. One of the tunes opens with an actual fragment (all I can remember) of a folk-tune which in boyhood I heard a farm hand sing. I fear the tune itself is lost, as I have revisited the district to find that the singer is dead and that no one else in the "countryside" knows the song. I forbear for the present to say which Carol this is, as I shall be interested to know whether it will be readily identified by any folk-song expert, and whether—in that event—it will be too apparent where the folk-tune leaves off and my own begins. All the tunes can be sung, if required, in unison except " Tryste Noel," which, although included in the collection, is better described as a Christmas song than as a carol. I have the approval of the authoress for the sudden change from modal to modern idiom, to express the half passionate, half wistful appeal of the last two lines in each verse.

R. R. T.

November, 1912.   6281

TRYSTE NOEL.

A Song for Christmastide.

Words by
L. N. GUINEY.

R. R. TERRY.

5

JOSEPH AND THE ANGEL.

R. R. TERRY.

Allegretto. ♩.= 98.

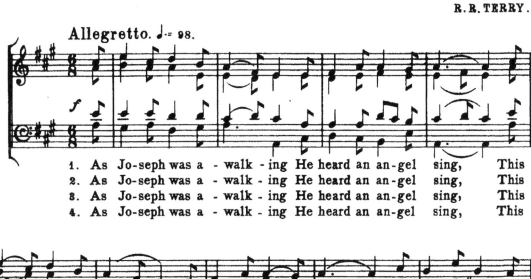

1. As Jo-seph was a - walk - ing He heard an an-gel sing, This
2. As Jo-seph was a - walk - ing He heard an an-gel sing, This
3. As Jo-seph was a - walk - ing He heard an an-gel sing, This
4. As Jo-seph was a - walk - ing He heard an an-gel sing, This

night shall be born Our hea - venly King. He nei-ther shall be
night shall be born Our hea - venly King. He nei-ther shall be
night shall be born Our hea - venly King. He nei-ther shall be
night shall be born Our hea - venly King. He nei-ther shall be

born In hou - sen nor in hall, Nor in the place of
cloth - ed In pur - ple nor in pall, But all in fair
rock - ed In sil - ver nor in gold, But in a wood - en
chris-ten-ed In white wine nor in red, But in the fair spring

Pa - ra - dise, But in an ox - 's stall. No - el No - el.
lin - en As wear ba - bies all. No - el No - el.
cra - dle That rocks on the mould. No - el No - el.
wa - ter As we were christen - ed. No - el No - el.

SO BLYSSID BE THE TYME.

R. R. TERRY.

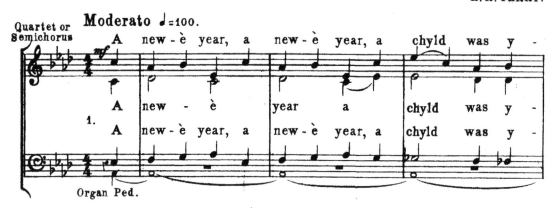

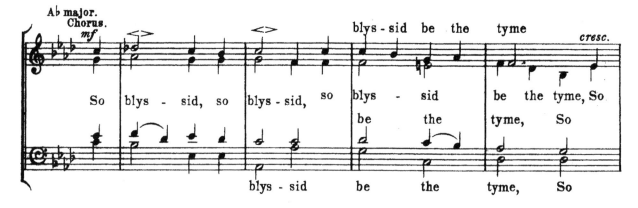

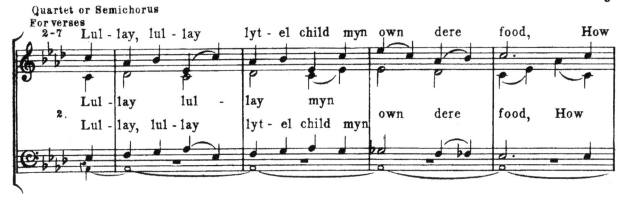

Quartet or Semichorus
For verses

Lul - lay, lul - lay   lyt - el child myn own   dere   food,   How

Lul - lay   lul - lay   myn

2.

Lul - lay, lul - lay   lyt - el child myn own   dere   food,   How

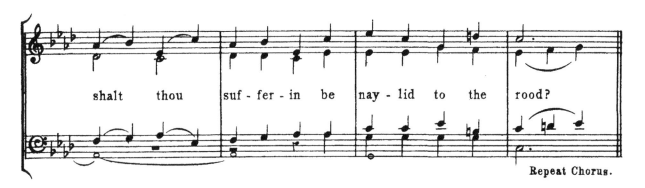

shalt   thou   suf - fer - in   be   nay - lid   to   the   rood?

Repeat Chorus.

3.

Lullay, lullay, lytel child, myn own dere smerte,
How shalt thou sufferin the scharpe spear to thi herte?
So blyssid be the tyme!

4.

Lullay, lullay, lytel child, I singe al for thi sake,
Many a one the scharpe scar to thi body is shape
So blyssid be the tyme!

5.

Lullay, lullay, lytel child, fayre happis thee befalle,
How shalt thou sufferin to drink ezel and galle?
So blyssid be the tyme!

6.

Lullay, lullay, lytel child, I sing all beforn,
How shalt thou sufferin the scharpe garlong of thorn?
So blyssid be the tyme!

7.

Lullay, lullay, lytel child, why weepy thou so sore?
Thou art bothin God and man, what woldest thou be more?
So blyssid be the tyme!

THE KING'S BIRTHDAY.

R. R. TERRY.

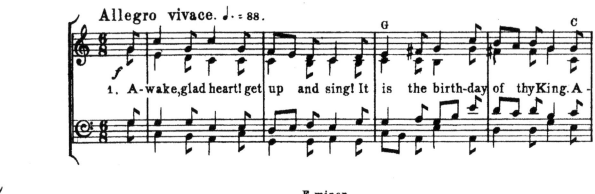

Allegro vivace. ♩. = 88.

1. A-wake, glad heart! get up and sing! It is the birth-day of thy King. A-

-wake! A-wake! The sun doth shake Light from his locks, and all the way Breathing per-fumes, doth

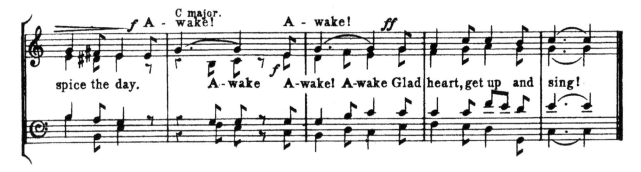

spice the day. A-wake! A-wake A-wake! A-wake Glad heart, get up and sing!

2.
Awake! awake! hark how th'wood rings,
Winds whisper, and the busy springs
    A concert make;
    Awake! awake!
Man is their high priest, and should rise
To offer up the sacrifice.
    Awake! awake!
    Glad heart, get up and sing!

3.
I would I were some bird or star,
Flutt'ring in woods, or lifted far
    Above this inn
    And road of sin!
Then either star or bird should be
Shining or singing still to thee.
    Awake! awake!
    Glad heart, get up and sing!

CHRIST WAS BORN ON CHRISTMAS DAY.

R.R. TERRY.

3.
Let the bright red berries glow
Everywhere in goodly show;
Christus natus hodie:
The babe, the Son, the Holy One of Mary.

4.
Christian men, rejoice and sing
'Tis the birthday of a King,
Ex Maria virgine:
The God, the Lord, by all adored for ever.

LULLAY, LULLAY.

R.R.TERRY.

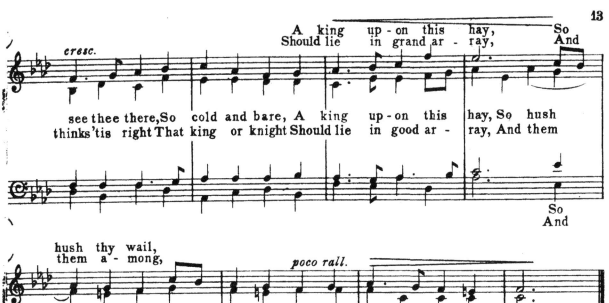

4.

"My mother Mary thine I be,
  Though I be laid in stall,
Both lords and dukes shall worship me,
  And so shall monarchs all.
    Thou shalt well see
    That princes three
  Shall come on the twelfth day,
    Then let me rest
    Upon thy breast
  And sing lullay, lullay."

5.

"Now tell me sweetest Lord I pray,
  Thou art my love and dear,
How shall I nurse thee to thy mind,
  And make thee glad of cheer.
    For all thy will
    I will fulfil,
  I need no more to say,
    And for all this,
    I will thee kiss
  And sing lullay, lullay."

6.

"My mother dear, when time it be,
  Then take me up aloft
And set me up upon thy knee,
  And handle me full soft,
    And in thy arm
    Thou wilt me warm
  And keep me night and day,
    And if I weep
    And may not sleep,
  Thou'lt sing lullay, lullay."

7.

"Now sweetest Lord, since it is so
  That thou art most of might,
I pray thee grant a boon to me
  If it be meet and right,
    That child or man
    That will or can
  Be merry on this day
    To bliss them bring
    And I shall sing
  Lullay, lullay, lullay."

THE ANGEL GABRIEL.

R. R. TERRY.

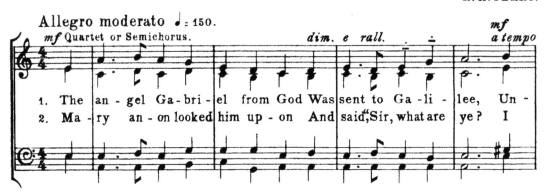

Allegro moderato ♩ = 150.

mf Quartet or Semichorus.   *dim. e rall.*   *mf a tempo*

1. The an - gel Ga - bri - el from God Was sent to Ga - li - lee, Un -
2. Ma - ry an - on looked him up - on And said, "Sir, what are ye? I

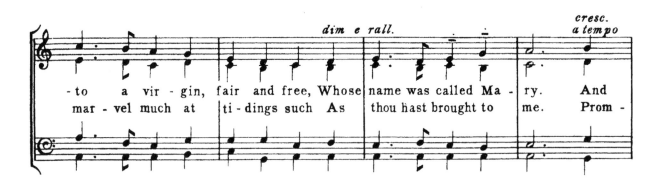

dim e rall.   *cresc. a tempo*

- to a vir - gin, fair and free, Whose name was called Ma - ry. And
mar - vel much at ti - dings such As thou hast brought to me. And Prom -

dim.

when the an - gel thi - ther came He fell down on his knee, And
- ised I am to Jo - seph So fell the lot to me: There -

dim. e rall. molto.   *p*

look - ing on the vir - gin's face Said, "Hail, all hail, Ma - ry."
- fore I pray de - part a - way, I stand in doubt of thee."

N.B. A very pronounced dim. e rall. to be made on the chords marked ⁝

Then sing we all, both great and small, No - el, No - el, No - el. We

molto rall.

may re - joice to hear the voice Of an - gel Ga - bri - el.

3.

"Mary," he said, "be not afraid
 And now believe in me,
The power of God, the Holy Ghost,
 Shall overshadow thee.
Thou shalt conceive, but not to grieve
 As the Lord told to me;
God's own dear Son from heaven shall come
 And shalt be born of thee."
 Then sing we all, etc.

4.

This came to pass as God's will was
 E'en as the angel told.
About midnight an angel bright
 Came to the shepherd's fold,
And told them then both where and when
 Born was the child our Lord,
And all along this was their song
 "All glory be to God".
 Then sing we all, etc.

5.

Good people all, both great and small
 The which do hear my voice,
With one accord let's praise the Lord
 And in our hearts rejoice;
In love abound to all around
 While we our lifetime spend,
While we have space let's pray for grace
 So let my carol end.
 Then sing we all, etc.

MYN LYKING.

R.R.TERRY.

Fine. mf

2. That

mf a tempo

Fine.

cresc. rall. D.C. 𝄉 al Fine.

2. same Lord is he that made al-lé thing Of al-lé lordis He is Lord of al-lé kynges Kyng.

mf cresc. rall.

cresc. molto rall. D.C. 𝄉 al Fine.

3. There was mickle melody at that chyl-des birth. All that were in heav'nly bliss, they made mickle mirth.

mf cresc. molto rall.

cresc. molto rit. D.C. 𝄉 al Fine.

4. Angels bright sang their song to that chyld; Blyssid be thou, and so be she, so meek and so mild.

mf cresc. molto rit.

I SING OF A MAYDEN.

R.R.TERRY.

2.

He came all so stillé
To his mother's bower,
As dew in Aprillé
That fall'th on the flower.
He came all so stillé
There his mother lay,
As dew in Aprillé
That fall'th on the spray.

REGINA CELI LETARE.

R.R.TERRY.

Moderato ♩.=84.

1. Ho - ly may - den blys-sid thou be, God - es sonne is
2. Hail wyfe, hail may - den, hail bride of bliss, Hail daughter hail sister hail
3. Thou art empress of hea-ven so free, Wor - thy mayden in

born of thee, The fa - ther of hea - ven wor - ship we, ⎫
full of pi - tē, Hail cho - sen to the per - son-ys three ⎬ Re -
ma - jes - tē, Now wor - ship we the tren - y - tē, ⎭

gi - na ce - li, le - ta - re, Re - gi - na ce - li le - ta - re.

4.

So gracious, so precious in ryalté,
Thus gentyl, thus good, thus finde we,
There is non such in non countré,
Regina celi, letare.

5.

And therefore kneel we down on our knee,
This blyssid birth worshipe we,
This is a song of humyleté,
Regina celi, letare.

WHEN CHRIST WAS BORN.

R.R.TERRY.

THE NEW YEAR.

R. R. TERRY.

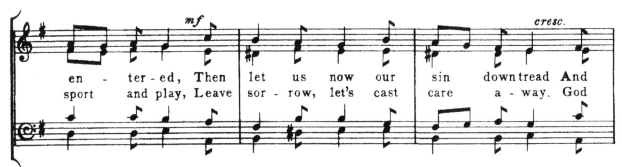

3.
And now with new year's gifts each friend
Unto each other they do send;
God grant we may our lives amend
And that the truth may appear.

4.
Now like the snake cast off your skin
Of evil thoughts and wicked sin,
And to amend this year begin.
God send you a merry new year.

The Curwen Edition
A Selection of Recent Issues

		Voices	Staff	S-f
EDGAR L. BAINTON. OPERETTA.				
3558	Walooki the Bear	Unis	1/– both	
PART-SONGS.				
61046	Autumn in the orchard	SCTB	3d	1½d
60962	Ballad of Semmerwater, The	SCTB	3d	1d
71457	Blow, bugle, blow	SSCC	3d	1½d
71362	Cloud, The	Unis	2d	1d
61025	Clown's Courtship, The	SCTB	3d	1½d
61024	Federal Song, A	SCTB	3d	2d
71398	There is sweet music	SC	2d	1d
ANTHEM.				
80549	Heavens declare the glory	SCTB	4d	
PERCY C. BUCK. PART-SONGS.				
71515	Babes in the Wood	SC	3d	1½d
71200	Ballad of Mary Jane, The	SS	3d	1d
71516	Christmas Dawn	SS	2d	1½d
71072	Harbour Song	SC	2d	1d
71255	Mister Nobody	SC	2d	1½d
71254	Phillis	SS	2d	1d
71073	Ternary of Littles, A	SS	2d	1d
71201	To a child embracing his mother	SS	2d	1d
E. T. DAVIES. PART-SONGS.				
71396	Autumn Days	SC	3d	1½d
50562	Gentle Dove (Y Deryn Pur)	TTBB	4d	2d
61013	When summer's merry days come	SCTB	3d	1½d
50535	Winds, The	TTBB	3d	2d
LEARMONT DRYSDALE. PART-SONGS.				
60797	Barbara Allan	SCTB	4d	2d
71060	Wha daur meddle wi' me ?	SC	2d	1d
THOMAS F. DUNHILL. PIANOFORTE.				
9172	Old-World Measure, An		1/–	
9161	Rigaudon		1/–	
9162	Sylphides		1/–	
9173	Tripping round the Maypole		1/–	
9163	Valse Plaintive		1/–	
PART-SONG.				
71463	Owl, The	Unis	2d	1d
ERNEST FARRAR. ANTHEMS.				
80577	Almighty God	SATB	2d	1d
50534	They that put their trust	TB	3d	

LONDON : J. CURWEN & SONS LTD., 24 BERNERS ST., W.1

CURWEN EDITION

A Selection of Recent Issues

G. T. HOLST PART-SONGS AND ARRANGEMENTS

61113	Bring us in good ale	SCTB	6d	3d
50542	Dirge for two veterans, A	TTBB	6d	4d
71517	Dream of Christmas, A	SS	4d	2d
61087	I love my love (arrangement)	SCTB	6d	4d
61083	I sowed the seeds of love (arrangement)	SCTB	4d	3d
61085	Matthew, Mark, Luke, and John (arrangement)	SCTB	4d	3d
61086	Song of the Blacksmith, The (arrangement)	SCTB	6d	4d
71458	Swallow leaves her nest, The	SSC	4d	2d
61088	Swansea Town (arrangement)	SCTB	6d	6d
61084	There was a tree (arrangement)	SCTB	6d	4d
71632	I vow to thee my country	Unis	4d	*
71655	Christmas Song	Unis	4d	*
61190	Evening watch	SCTB	6d	
50617	I love my love	TTBB	6d	*
71654	I saw three ships	Unis	4d	4d
50619	I sowed the seed of love	TTBB	4d	3d
71656	Masters in this hall	Unis	4d	
50616	Matthew, Mark, Luke, and John	TTBB	4d	3d
50618	Song of the Blacksmith	TTBB	6d	3d
50615	Swansea Town	TTBB	6d	4d

CAROLS

80589	Lullay, my liking	SATB	4d	4d
80590	Of one that is so fair	SATB	4d	

OPERA

3651 Savitri Vocal Score 10/–; Full Score, (90765) 42/– net, Orch. Matl. on hire

FULL ORCHESTRA

90761 Beni Mora, Oriental Suite in E minor, Score, 21/– net; Parts, 21/– net; Ex. Vn., each 2/– net; Ex. Vl. & C., each 1/6 net; Ex. Bass, each 1/– net.

90725 The Planets, Suite for large orchestra, Score, 63/– net; Miniature, 10/– net; Parts on hire, Cho. parts, each 6d. net.

STRING ORCHESTRA

90718 St. Paul's Suite, Score, 7/6 net; Parts, each 1/6 net.

VIOLIN SOLOS

94027	Intermezzo (from St. Paul's Suite)	2/6
94026	Jig (from St. Paul's Suite)	2/6

PIANO SOLO

99035	Toccata (Newburn Lads')	2/6

PIANO TRANSCRIPTION

99036	Beni Mora	4/–
99022	Planets Transcription for pfte. (four hands), by Vally Lasker and Nora Day	10/–
99024	St. Paul's Suite. Piano transcription by Vally Lasker	3/–

ALBERT W. KETELBEY ORCHESTRAL

90705 Canzonetta. Parts, 6d. net cash each; Piano-Conductor ... 1/– net

A. MADELEY RICHARDSON PART-SONGS

71152	Bid me discourse	SC	6d	3d
71154	Break, break, break	SSC	6d	2d
71120	It was a lover and his lass	SC	6d	2d
71204	Lark now leaves, The	SSC	6d	3d
71119	My true love hath my heart	SC	6d	2d
71121	O mistress mine	SC	6d	2d
71150	Philomel	SSC	4d	2d
71118	Under the greenwood tree	SSC	6d	2d
71151	Weep you no more, sad fountains	SSC	6d	2d
50433	Wet sheet and a flowing sea, A	ATTBB	6d	4d

ANTHEMS

50431	I was glad when they said	TTBB	6d	4d
71234	O God, Thou art my God	SC	4d	2d